Jimmy & Rita

Poems by
Kim Addonizio

BOA Editions, Ltd. • Rochester, NY • 1997

LC #: 96–83953
ISBN: 1–880238–41–1 paper

First Edition
97 98 99 00   7 6 5 4 3 2 1

Publications by BOA Editions, Ltd.—
a not-for-profit corporation under section 501 (c) (3)
of the United States Internal Revenue Code—
are made possible with the assistance of grants from
the Literature Program of the New York State Council on the Arts,
the Literature Program of the National Endowment for the Arts,
the Lannan Foundation,
the Eric Mathieu King Fund of The Academy of American Poets,
as well as from the Rochester Area Foundation Community Arts Fund
administered by the Arts & Cultural Council for Greater Rochester,
the County of Monroe, NY,
and from many individual supporters.

Cover Design: Daphne Poulin-Stofer
Cover Photo: Ina Campbell
Author Photo: Joe Allen
Typesetting: Richard Foerster
Manufacturing: McNaughton & Gunn, Lithographers
BOA Logo: Mirko

BOA Editions, Ltd.
A. Poulin, Jr., President
(1938–1996)
260 East Avenue
Rochester, NY 14604

for V

I'd rather die before I wake
like Marilyn Monroe
and you can throw my dreams out in the street
let the rain make 'em grow

—Tom Waits

Contents

PART ONE

December

For a while Rita works
at a massage parlor on Eddy Street.
All she has to do
is jerk them off, no
fucking or kissing.
She washes her hands seven,
eight times a day. Dreams
of scrubbing off skin,
red strips of it falling
into a sinkful of suds.
She buries what's left
of her hands in the white
froth, piled
like new snow
she would scoop out
as a child to make
a man.

Portrait

Of seven kids, Rita
was the oldest. She used to hide
from the noise in the house—
sliding down in the bathtub,
warm water in her ears.
If she hummed
her head filled up with music.
Her mother would be in bed,
yelling for her to bring something—
her medicine or a drink. The boys
had gunfights or watched TV.
Her baby sister stood in the playpen
crying to have her diaper changed.
If her father was home he might do it,
might even make them all
sit down together at the table
to eat. But that hardly ever happened.

Her father sold 8 x 10 portraits
from Golden West Photography,
door after door closing on him
in neighborhoods in Nevada—
places no one went
or came from. Rita has pictures
of herself at every age to twelve
in front of a velvet backdrop,
holding the latest baby,
smiling to please him.
On a run to Elko
his blue Dart quit
and he hitched to Vegas
leaving a seatful of coupons
(*Professional Full Color Portrait Only 99¢*)
and his briefcase of samples.

For a while they received letters
with twenties folded inside
(*Hope this will help. Love to All*),
postcards showing the lit
fountain at Caesar's Palace
or a line of chorus girls.
Then they moved to California.
The mail never caught up,
if there was any. Rita sent
a picture of herself
to the last motel address,
but it came back finally, a crease
wrinkling her best dress
and the sea behind her.

Days

Diane. Who gives me downers, loans me money. Sometimes dresses. Diane with the breasts men always stare at, that and her red hair. Once she shaved her head. She looked like a weasel or something, her eyes huge, maybe from the meth though. I think that's why she did it, just started cutting and got into it the way you do on meth. Afterwards she hardly went out, and then always with a hat on.

I come over in the afternoons. Diane lives in the apartment down the hall. The building is right behind the projects on Hayes Street. We both get checks but hers is more because she has a kid. I never see it, a little girl. She stays at her grandmother's outside San Jose. We watch all the soaps. Diane does meth and drinks vodka and I have some with cranberry juice, but only if I don't have any stuff. On junk I only want warm tea. Diane is always painting her toenails, black or purple or deep red. She has a rose tattoo on her stomach, butterfly on her shoulder. She wears a lot of makeup to hide her freckles. Her boyfriends buy her nice things. A bracelet, a black lace teddy. She tells me how bad they are in bed. Once I said they all are and she looked at me and said, Poor baby, you mean you never had a good man? How old are you? she said. I told her twenty-two. Diane is thirty-four, without her makeup she looks older but I've only seen her like that once.

I feel used up, she says. Do you know what that's like? Closing her eyes and lying back on her couch. I put my little finger in a cigarette burnhole. Diane goes into the kitchen and takes the vodka bottle from the freezer, all cloudy, brings it back and pours some for us. We sit there a while longer, then I get up to leave. She sits up straight and gives me a big smile and then slumps back down. Don't go yet, she says. So I sit on the arm of the couch and lean against her a little and we watch the six o'clock news, and then the sitcoms, and drink some more.

Party

Rita leans against someone's kitchen table.
Doesn't know a soul here except Diane,
who's listening to an old man—
sunglasses and a cigar, drunk—
I'm not trying to take you
to bed, but would I?
In a minute. In a minute.
Rita wishing she could just go home,
take a Valium, put on the TV.

Need a drink, pretty lady?
Jimmy slams the refrigerator and turns
to her, grinning.
Dark hair slicked back, blue eyes,
St.Christopher medal dangling.
His sweatshirt with the sleeves
cut off, tattoo on his right bicep—
cartoon devil riding a panther.
What's your name?
Slow look from top to bottom.
Rita closing her eyes
to decide, then opens them
and he's across the room,
his arm around a black girl.

Later Diane takes her into the bathroom,
hands her a rolled ten. Rita leans
to the toilet lid,
goes out with her head ringing
right up to him.
Rita, she says
and he repeats it
three times like a prayer:
Rita Rita Rita

Where you been all my life, girl?
(Nowhere.)
Her lips are numb, she almost
can't feel it when he kisses her.

Dead Men

One summer doing maintenance work
at a university, Jimmy's crew
had to move cadavers
for the medical school.
Chumley pulled a bag off,
said *Hey Jimmy!*
This here's your buddy, man.
Wake up and say hello, Chumley told
the corpse. He slipped a hammer
from his coveralls and whapped it
on the forehead, crunching bone.
Wake up, man, Chumley said,
then walked out
by the supply shed and got sick.
That was the easiest job,
Jimmy tells Rita. *They didn't*
make us do a damn thing else
all summer. I want to be
burned, my ashes scattered
from here to New Jersey.
I don't want no fucking assholes
to look at me.
Baby, I seen dead men.

Beer. Milk. The Dog. My Old Man.

My old man used to take the dog
out to the garage
where the poker game was
and set down a bowl
of beer, that's the kind of thing
he thought was funny. He used to
give me some too and laugh when I
threw up or fell over
a chair. He taught me to fight
by smacking the side of my head
with his open hand, calling me
a pussy. Don't let them give you
any shit he said. When he smacked
my mother she didn't hit back,
just yelled at him. Once she threw
a glass of milk at his head.
It hit the wall and broke
to pieces on the floor.

I was ten when he died.
Too young to figure it out.
What I thought about was the milk
on the kitchen floor that time,
how they'd both
left it there and gone to bed.
The dog got to it and swallowed glass.
My mother said the dog
just got sick. The milk
evaporated she said.
Meaning it just
went into the air.
I thought, how could something
be there and then not? Milk.
The dog. My old man. He loved

a cold beer. Sometimes I'd sit up
at night in the garage and watch
how he drank it, tipping his head
way back, and I'd try to drink mine
exactly the same,
but quietly, so he wouldn't notice
and send me away.

Blackberry

What is it about her?
That she's pretty.
She's too thin,
all bones and angles,
and small tits. Though the nipples
are long. Honeysuckle tips.
She likes him to bite them
but he never does it as hard
as she wants. *I won't break,*
she says, when he holds her.
But he isn't sure.
When he's alone
she's there, an ache.
He stays away for days
hoping it will stop.
Then he shows up
at her place, and she unlocks
the chain. *Jimmy.*
I missed you.
Her nervous smile.
Her mouth. Red lipstick
he likes the taste of.
Blackberry, it's called.
He goes around all day
with that word in his head.

Fixing

watching it boil in the spoon then Jimmy
draws it up for me flicks the cylinder
with his finger to get the air
bubbles out his belt's around
my arm, buckle dug into my skin

the needle sliding in, my blood
outside of me then coming back sweeter
the first rush and his cologne smell hitting me
together he pulls back the plunger his hands
are steady pushing it in again I lost

my glass needle it's better than
the plastic ones but Jimmy's good
he's so good like that again please
I look down at my arm the
tiny new mark the older ones I cover

with my hand but he doesn't notice
he's cleaning the needle squirting
water across the table at me *Did you*
like that he says I let my head fall back
close my eyes yes Jimmy you're so

Ocean Beach

They take the streetcar to the end of the line,
spread a blanket, unwrap sandwiches.
Jimmy pops a canned margarita
and gives it to Diane. Rita lights
a joint and passes it. Gulls floating by,
sanderlings at the edge of the water
running up and then back
when the waves come in.
Diane says *Birds*
are spirit messengers.
That's the kind of thing
she says all the time. She believes
in mindreading, too. Jimmy says
Give me a break, but smiles.
It's one of those rare days
when the city is actually hot.
Everyone out on a Tuesday afternoon.
Rita wonders who the other people are,
where they'll go back to tonight.
She doesn't want to leave. It's too good
being stoned, a little drunk,
lying against Jimmy with her eyes closed.
His hand in her hair, smell
of his sweat, the heat pressing down.
Voices, a faint salt breeze. No one
to bother them. *Hey seagull,*
Jimmy says. *Got any messages for me?*
Diane laughing. The sound
of wings. Or maybe, falling
asleep, she just imagines them.

Moving In

Jimmy brings over a few boxes.
Albums, clothes, *KO* magazines,
six-ounce boxing gloves, his high school diploma.
Framed newspaper photo of the Chacon-Limon fight.
Seven Marine Band harmonicas,
red coleus he found in a dumpster.
Rita makes room in the closet,
watches him hang shirts
next to her dresses.
That afternoon they make love
on the living room rug,
finishing a bottle
of Jim Beam.
Jimmy wakes up at dusk,
stares at the couch legs, confused
for a few seconds.
Lights a Camel, watches
rings rising to the ceiling.
He hates this time of day,
feels death coming on like a punch
he won't duck in time.
Each circle of smoke
solid at first
then pulling itself apart.

Jimmy's Boxing Career

Got started too late
to be serious about it.
24 years old
hanging around the gym
hitting the speed bag.
His hands small, like LaMotta's.
A few bouts
in the N.J. Policeman's League,
one of three whites.
Fought black guys
heavier, stronger.
Didn't beat anybody.
But fought them.
One thing he's proud of.

Round

Rita misses the vein,
massages the lump
that comes up.
She rolls her sleeve back down.
Jimmy watches the boxers on TV
bloody each other, one
on the ropes, shaking sweat off
like a dog under a hose.
Let's get married, Rita says.
She puts her head in Jimmy's lap,
nuzzles his balls
through his underwear.
The guy on the ropes goes down.
He pushes her away. Her voice
in his ear now, drowning out
the count. *Marry me. Jimmy.*
He sees the crowd
on its feet, screaming,
him just lying there.

Starlight

Ten p.m. walking past the Greyhound station on Seventh Street. Bums curled in every doorway. Rita's high heels loud, the silence following her like a man with a knife. *Do what I tell you.* Until she's running, past the Jack In The Box, lit up, inside solitary men hunched over coffee, torn sugar packets on plastic trays, black girls in striped uniforms. The Embassy Theater posters, *DAMES*, *TASTE OF PINK*, a girl with green hair in the glassed-in booth reading a magazine, Madonna on the cover. Into the Starlight Room where Jimmy's supposed to be. At the round bar two men are playing dice with the bartender. Rita orders gin and Seven Up. The room is round, too, no corners, mural of the city curving along one wall. Cords of strung white lights blinking above her. Three drinks later she swears she's turning, points a finger at the Golden Gate until it shifts out of range. Turquoise glow above the painted hills. Out of money now. Slam of the dice cup. The carousel spinning her. Her father holding her red coat and doll, plastic pinwheel she won at the penny toss. Blurring as she goes by. She lays her cheek on the bar, the reins loose in her hands.

Five A.M.

it's not the worst time to wake up
sometimes it's four a.m., earlier
then I know I'll be sick the whole day

get up to puke in the toilet
Sattiva the black and white cat
follows me in
puts her paws up looks into the bowl

some guy in the bed I don't know, Jimmy's
out of town I get lonely, easy
to find someone to buy drinks
The Embers The Town Pump or Dick's
doing shooters and listening, they always want
to talk at you blah-de-blah

I feel my way down the hall
take Nuprin with some flat Coke
stand in the middle of the kitchen
moonlight on the dirty dishes
my hair stinking of smoke
my nakedness I can't
take off, get rid of
flush down some hole

go back to bed and curl
away from him
wait for the numbers on the clock-radio
to flip forward to morning

Trenton

His mother is thin from the cancer,
but her stomach's the size
of a watermelon.
Nights holding her
until the pills work
he looks out at the south wall
of the prison across the street,
wonders why he never did time.
(Chumley busted on Morningside
after copping in Harlem,
Jimmy in the back seat
not holding anything.
Or that time hitting up
with Pedro the Puerto Rican nurse
in an Arco bathroom in the Bronx,
cops pounding on the door,
You lucky son of a bitch
heard all his life.)

Freezing storm outside.
The window's starting to ice.
He lies back on the couch,
lets himself float out
past Bingo's and Quinn's,
past the Treasure Chest,
strip joint where the P.R.'s watch
women with tattoos on their asses—
past all that crap
to his old man's grave.
Look at me you dumb fuck
At least you're still alive
Rain filling the letters
of his name.

Orchids

No good bars left in Trenton.
All his friends moved out or dead.
Sitting in Quinn's, remembering
Hawaiian Night at Bucchi's Harmonica Bar—
girls in grass skirts doing the hula,
the bartender knowing him, guys saying
How's it going, Jimbo?
and the bead curtains to the back room
where the ice machine was and a girl
once took a cube in her mouth,
ran it cold down his belly.

Walking back to his mother's
he sees one black whore
working the corner,
but she isn't very pretty.
Somebody smashed the windows in Bingo's.
His mother wakes
in the middle of the night and calls out.
He comes to, feeling that ice
sliding down his thighs,
still smelling the flowers, her hair.

What Happened

She's waiting at the Greyhound station
when he gets off the bus. The place smells
of piss, like the hospital room
(those volunteers in blue uniforms
and teddy-bear pins
saying *We've seen miracles here*).
Rita standing there, her hair damp
from washing it. *Welcome home.* He thinks
of the empty apartment, his aunt
trying on his mother's clothes to see
what she'd keep. That last
afternoon he sat beside her body
staring at the bed rails. Then out
to the cold air of the parking lot.
Driving his cousin's car
to Quinn's and waking up
in the back seat late that night,
one eye puffed up, his palms gravel-scraped
and bleeding. *What happened?*
Rita asks, touching his face.
Nothing. I don't know.
He starts crying. Hurries her outside
and walks fast ahead of her.

Jimmy's Birthday

What could happen:
car accident bar fight some crazy
with a gun or bus out of control
rocketing over the curb
(Jerry Lee blinded by a pool cue
Frank with his father's .22
his toe on the trigger).
Never thought he'd make thirty
but here he is,
head tipped back to the bar
and Chumley shooting tequila
burning down his throat. The band
playing heavy blues. How he'd love
to slip the harp from his back pocket
and blow, hands cupped
around the microphone.
But people might think
he's no good (*Who is this fag?*)
or just not listen. Fuck them.
Someday he'll knock
their socks off.

There's my ex-old lady
with a niggah,
Chumley says, heads out
the swinging door. Jimmy following
dizzy, hit when it swings back.
Chumley's down by a Cadillac,
his switchblade jammed in a tire.
Man, don't do that,
grabbing him around the waist,
the two of them rolling
and coming up bloody,
knife flipping closed and opening

Chumley's hand. Then they're running
and in the car, headed the wrong way
down Franklin. Jimmy thinking
Why aren't I scared?
Chumley veering away from horns and headlights.
Later that night
after Chumley is bandaged in napkins
crashed on their couch, Jimmy turns
to Rita's naked back
and starts shaking. *Hold me,*
he says, but she's asleep
and he doesn't repeat it.

Fairmont

Rita's first time in San Francisco—
seventeen years old,
with her brothers Jack and Charlie
at the bottom of Powell Street, trying
to buy Quaaludes. They went off
down Market and she rode the cable car
to the top. She wanted to see
the Fairmont Hotel.
White limo in front,
the doorman in his uniform.
She felt shy sitting
in the lobby, in her torn jeans
and black sweater, but nobody
paid any attention. Except one man,
blonde hair and a grey suit,
who offered a drink
(*I can't, I'm too young*)
and then fifty if she'd go
somewhere with him.
He took her across the street
to an office building, into
a tiny bathroom, fucked her
over the toilet. Then he left—
to get his wallet, he said.
Rita waited, then walked out
down a red-carpeted hall, past
two receptionists. Crying
even in the crowded elevator.
Back at the turnaround
she found her brothers,
gagged down two pills
without water.
Where'd you go? Jack asked.
Rita wouldn't say. She knew

they'd tell her she was stupid
not to get the money first.
They sat down by Woolworth's.
Music from a saxophone loud
in their ears. Rita waiting
until the shame went away
and the other girl came,
the one with the same name,
but no memories.

What Jimmy Remembers

Girls in white stockings and checkered wool jumpers, round white collars, red bows at their throats. Birds in Saint Christopher's schoolyard—hundreds of them, black, spread out across the lawn in late afternoon. The brick wall of the steel mill on Dye Street he could see from the living room window, his father in there working, his mother in a shiny black dress coming in at dawn after singing in some nightclub, waking him for school. Shivering and dressing over the heating vent in the front hall. Dark-blue blazer and black shoes. A puppy that died of distemper, put in a shopping bag and into a can in Bushler's Alley. Cotton candy on the boardwalk in Seaside Heights, the barkers calling *Hey bub, Hey sonny, Buster, Skip, You.* Mickey the Waffle-Whiffer, old retarded guy they used to tease by dropping pennies into his coffee at the Meatball Cafe. Stickball in the streets. Touching Mary Prinski's left breast, just the underside of it, not even getting to the nipple but that was enough. The black hearse carrying his father through the snow, a semicircle of metal folding chairs. The green faces in avocado leaves smiling down at him. God in the clouds. *Who art in Heaven.* His mother, ghost now: wearing a stolen mink, flipping a cigarette from a deck of Lucky's. His father moving towards her with a match, cupping his palms around the flame.

Her Voice

Jimmy bruised two ribs
fighting with Chumley on his birthday.
Days on the couch,
light sliced thin through the blinds,
feeling like a truck is backed
onto his chest.
Rita working some convention
standing around in a short skirt
and cowboy boots. One evening
she brings a baggie of cold ribs
and says they're replacements.

He wakes up nights sure
he's dying, the air close,
panic making it harder
just to breathe.
She talks him down,
her voice a tide
carrying him in
and for once
he doesn't resist it.

PART TWO

Listening To Jimmy

Rita's got her bare foot
in the ice around the keg.
The party's too loud in there—
she likes sitting on this railing
looking up at the ringed moon,
her foot going numb.
She can hear Jimmy
telling stories in the kitchen.
How Chumley shot a cop's son
in Trenton, the woman
with FUCK tattooed on her tongue
who ripped him off for dope.
New Jersey stories. Before
California, before Rita knew him.
Jimmy starts laughing
at something another woman says.
Rita in her beige wedding dress
and brown gardenia, shoes
and stockings lost somewhere—
maybe the van they rode in
from the courthouse, or the bar
they got thrown out of. Some drunk
trying to paw Rita, Jimmy saying
That's my wife and hitting him.
She feels queasy—champagne
always does that. Rita shivers
at a shooting star, falling
over the houses
to their end—parking lot,
dunes, the sea: dark tablecloth
cleaned of crumbs.

Honeymoon

Rita wakes and puts her hand
to the bus window.
Outside, black pines and snow.
Jimmy's head on her shoulder.
The window is cold; she wishes
the driver would stop right now
in the middle of night and nowhere
so she could get out and see her breath,
take a handful of white powder
and put it to her lips.
How long has it been
since she did that? Mittens
on her hands, crystals of ice
caught in the wool. Her toes numb
and then tingling when she went inside.
She stays awake for an hour,
watching the trees,
mile after mile of them.

The dawn is gray, a few flakes
swirling down. They find
the motel, get a key to their cabin.
Jimmy's boots crack ice
on the front porch. In the yard
Rita tilts her head back,
sticks out her tongue and turns around
and around. Jimmy calls out
there's a fireplace inside.
When she goes in he's standing
naked in front of the fire.
She goes over to him. He kneels
and pulls down her jeans,
underwear. His mouth
against her. Her hand in his hair.

The snow coming down faster,
laying a thin cover over
the cluster of cabins,
starting to soften the edges of things.

Deliveries

Once Chumley found a drunk
in a garbage can,
rolled him all the way
down Hancock Street.
At the bottom
Chumley knocked on the can.
Come in, the drunk said.
That's how Jimmy feels.
They kick your ass
and you're still polite.
His boss has it in
for him, won't let up.
Fuck this job. But he needs
the money. Won't listen
to Chumley saying *Got*
a little proposition for you.
Dope or forgery.
Jimmy's scared shitless
of getting caught
(as a kid he played
on the strip of grass
next to the prison wall,
under the coils of barbed wire,
feeling secure; no one
could escape).
Anyway he doesn't mind the driving
so much. Running
into garages with gaskets,
piston rings, brake shoes.
Sometimes a good-looking girl
in the office, and calendars
with women sprawled over hoods.
It's just his fucking boss.
Sometimes Jimmy sneaks in

to the office when it's empty,
his heart racing, and takes
something. A parts manual
he drops in a trash can
going home. A ball-point pen
with a girl in a bathing suit
on it. Turn it upside down
and she's naked. He feels good,
driving around all day
with that in his pocket.

Blackouts

Jimmy says don't worry it's all there somewhere
do I remember the TV the basketball game was on
I acted normal he said smoked 2 cigarettes
didn't slur or fall down
I've never been a sloppy drunk
folded my clothes before bed
afraid to ask him if we made love
lay there after he left
for work, looking at my body
and couldn't tell

Company

I heard them coming up. I knew they were drunk, I pulled out the extra chair and sat down and waited. They had beers in their hands. Jimmy lifted my hair from my neck and started kissing me, I got up to make some tea and he followed me. Chumley traced the circle on the table his bottle made. Jimmy was talking but not making any sense, the words came out fast and garbled like another language. What? I said. He started throwing punches like there was somebody there. I wondered if he saw the things I see sometimes, not really people just shapes from the corner of my eye. Chumley kept busting out laughing. Jimmy fell on his knees and started kissing my foot through my sock. Please, Jimmy, I said. Wait until the company leaves. Chumley took off. I lit a cigarette and leaned against the doorframe and wondered if he'd start in on me again, but he just cleared the table with his hand and crawled on top of it and passed out. I put a blanket over him and went to bed. Now it's almost morning. I've been nodding from the junk all night and haven't slept. The shapes are disappearing from the corners of the room, moving out into the fog.

Silk

Rita. You ever think about dying?

I don't like to. (Sometimes she looks at schoolgirls on the bus, their bare knees, their makeup, and thinks: *You, too.*)

I think about it. Every fucking day.

You want me to rub your shoulders?

No. Did I ever tell you about my cousin who got shot trying to rip somebody off for drugs? He got into his taxi—that's what he did, drove a cab in Florida—and drove to a shopping mall and bled to death in the parking lot.

Shit, Jimmy, why do you tell me stuff like that? You're always talking about the bad things.

It just bothers me. Thinking about him dying like that.

Don't think about it, then.

Christ, Rita.

Diane told me once to imagine a bird holding a silk scarf in its beak and brushing it across the top of a mountain. As long as it takes the scarf to wear down the mountain, that's how many times we come back.

You believe that?

I'm just telling you what Diane said.

I don't think we come back, ever. It's a one-way ticket. So fuck it. (The girl who dragged her hair lightly across his chest. Blues harmonica. That was another life. Dying inside again and again. She would wear him down to nothingness.) Rita.

Mm.

Let's not die.

Go to sleep, baby. We won't.

My Name

Jimmy inside me coming and saying *Rita*
if my name is me if it's not
if I am or if I'm nothing empty
solid for that one moment

Main Event

I keep seeing the red gloves.
Not raised, just hanging there.
By his sides. This was
the other guy.
Rodriguez or some spic name.
Then the white square
under the lights.
Rita bugging me with questions,
me brushing her off.
Trying to watch the fight,
trying not to think about my boss
handing me my check
and saying *Get the hell out.*
Then those two quick jabs
to the head, and the ref asking
was he all right—the first guy.
The one who staggered and then
whammed onto the canvas.
I can't see the doctor
too good,
just his right hand
over the oxygen mask.
It's weird, what sticks.
Because then,
remembering it, I don't
see anything, not
the guy carried out
on a stretcher, though I know
he was. I forget the crowd
and just see the empty auditorium
and that blonde in the pink
one-piece bathing suit
walking around in her high heels,
holding the numbered cards

for each round.
I see her tits
and think Man,
I'd like to have them
swaying over me tonight.

Race

Jimmy dropped $200 at the track.
Should have bet Nickel Dancer
to win in the fourth—
one more regret to face down
late at night.
She pulls ahead
in a series of slow-motion strides.
In a dream he's riding her, sliding down
out of the saddle, dragged after.
Mud and shit in his face.
Rita's in the upstairs bar
letting that jockey they met
buy her drinks. Gold chains
and a diamond-eyed unicorn
around his scrawny neck.
Bullshitting about horses he'd owned,
his arm loose around her shoulders.
Jimmy wakes up and wants
to hit her, lying there curled
towards the window.
Just once,
hard,
so she'd cry out
and he could comfort her.

Watch

I wake up on someone's couch it's dark only a little moon through the window my skin cool and hot a man on me trying to push it in I'm too wasted I just let him he doesn't take very long. He gets off me and goes back through a door. I pull down my skirt go out to the street

walk blocks and blocks

a park huge dark trees men asleep on concrete benches

black woman in a leather miniskirt and silver boots asks me for a light. A car comes slow around the corner two men looking at us.

I start running finally I'm back at the apartment Jimmy's not there. I try to think if he was with me earlier. I've lost my keys. Ring Diane's buzzer she lets me in and gives me the extra set. In bed I try to sleep but the vomit comes up and I go to the bathroom and throw up then get under the cool shower water. I bring a pair of scissors back to bed. If I watch the door nothing will happen, no one will come. I curl up small and lie still trying not to breathe I guess I fall asleep because Jimmy wakes me taking the scissors from my hand.

Cat

Rita said the cat was freaking
her out, staring at her.
Get it out of here,
she said, *It's evil.*
It's just a fucking animal, I said.
It's just the dope, tomorrow
it will look different.
The next day I got up and Rita
was crouched in a corner, naked,
holding the broom in front of her.
I took it over to Chinatown
and let it go in an alley.
Today I saw one smashed
in the street
head and paws curled
belly split and oozing
but it was orange and white,
not ours,
and anyway I couldn't
do nothing about it. Jesus, it looked
like a baby, curled up
like that. A fucking cat.

Eviction

Waiting in line on Mission Street
an hour for a plate of salad
and a chili dog, then told
to hurry up and eat,
the line just as long
when they leave.
They come home to find everything
put out on the sidewalk.
A pile of clothes, the wilted coleus,
Rita's stuffed animals and jewelry.
Jimmy finds his leather pouch of harmonicas
but his cowboy boots are missing.
People passing, stopping to see
if they can take anything.
Don't look at us, he screams.
Punches the blue door
of the building, the pain
focusing him. The rest of the day
they panhandle,
get enough for a room
in the Tenderloin—two fags
in curlers in the lobby,
watching a bad TV
with a drooling old fuck
in a Forty-Niners jacket.
Rita hangs a printed cloth
over the window's iron grillwork.
Jimmy goes out. His fist still aches.
He's going to bury it in the face
of the first son-of-a-bitch
who looks at him sideways.

Room

Brown water in the sink,
an armchair of dishes.
Light cuts in
this time of day, flat
and hard. Rita
watches Jimmy sleep.
She likes the scar
below his left nipple,
a knife she thinks,
though he won't tell her.

Outside she can hear
the crazy woman screaming
Fuck Shit Piss,
and then stopping.
Jimmy sighs, his eyelids
trembling: dreams. The cloth
curtain lifts a little,
then falls. Rita feels good,
lying close to him,
watching the light begin
to spread and soften.
She touches the small scar—
underneath is his heart.
She lays her head there.
The room going dark.

Nightlife

Jimmy leans against a car door.
Loud thumping from a band
behind painted-over windows,
some warehouse on an alley
off Mission Street,
nobody here they know
and Diane never showed.
Rita empties a beer,
tosses it at a dumpster.

In the parking lot next door
someone crunches gravel,
broken glass.
Jimmy cold-shakes a baggie of speed,
the needle between his teeth.
Rita squeezes his arm with her thumbs.
The veins floating up.
Let go, Jimmy says.

Later in their room
he turns her over in bed.
Noise from upstairs,
plaster dusting loose from the ceiling.
The old guy, stumbling around drunk again.
Some punk he found on Polk Street
yelling about cigarettes. Jimmy trying
not to listen, kissing the back
of Rita's shoulder.

They unscrew wine and spread cheese
with a pocket knife.
Triangles of Laughing Cow on saltines.
Rita says *No one
can live like this for long.*

Jimmy grabs the knife
from her hand, jams it
in the wall. Pulls her
against him, twisting her arm back.
Haven't I been good to you? Jesus
fucking Christ I don't know
what you want

It's okay baby Rita says.
Let go, Jimmy
Let go

Weather

One morning he wasn't there. He was lying right beside me, breathing even, staring at the ceiling. I said Jimmy and he answered, we talked about how I was going to find a job or at least sell some food stamps so we could get something for our heads, the rain had been going on for days and we were both of us depressed. He said he'd go talk to Chumley's friend, maybe do a job for him, something pretty safe. And all the time I knew he wasn't there, and I couldn't say it. But he didn't know I knew, I could see that. So I got up and turned my back to him and got dressed and left him for a few hours to try and score.

Our Words

Trying not to drink so much Jimmy looks at me like he's disgusted he almost never comes back to the room anymore and when he does we fight. Tonight he left pissed, dented the refrigerator with his fist.

The TV's broke so I twist the plastic ice tray and fill a jar with gin and Schweppe's, pull a kitchen chair close to the radiator and the window. Nothing to eat but Fritos. Sick of them I throw handfuls into the street, boys hustling on the corner look up. Jimmy won't touch me anymore. Afraid he'll fall in. I'm a hole. Spilled ashtray out the window too. Then the bottle, smashing against the fire escape above the Vietnamese restaurant. Jimmy said they eat dog meat. Rats in the walls here, roaches spilling out of the kettle today when I poured water for tea. Neon cross of the Baptist church still blinks when I close my eyes. I'm sliding. Sticky. The door is jerked part-way open on its chain. Someone calling my name. (*Go away. I'm a hole.*) Jimmy kicks it open, six-pack hooked around his fingers slammed onto the table, his hands lifting me, dragging me to the bed. I can't hear our words. Somebody is shouting but I'm sinking. I'm deep, in the ocean with the fish. Their mouths moving. Their tails slap hard against my face, then they swim away.

Vincent

Sick of the rain, they take the bus to San Diego to see Vincent. Jimmy and Vincent had grown up together. Vincent was okay until high school, but then he started doing weird things—eating whole sticks of butter from the refrigerator, trying to hitchhike naked to Philadelphia. Vincent wrote Jimmy letters, and sent poems he'd made up—about not getting laid, about being caught jerking off in the institution. He'd be in Napa State for a year or so, and then better. He'd visit Jimmy, travel back east, end up in Napa again. Vincent was fat, and never washed, but he wasn't stingy. If he had money he'd help Jimmy out—meals, rent, a whore. Vincent was okay.

Vincent has a studio apartment with a tiny yard. It's the second week of February, most of his check's already gone. He's got a case of gin and a few cartons of cigarettes to get him through to the end of the month. He goes to confession at the church around the corner three and four times a day. The rest of the time he sits in a deck chair in the yard, watching people go by. Jimmy and Rita sprawl on his bed, fucked up on his medication, watching the soaps. Jimmy hadn't really wanted to bring her, but she cried, and he was afraid she'd do something stupid if he left her. And he felt bad for hitting her that night. Now things feel all right. The apartment is air-conditioned, every so often they look out through the curtain—an old sheet Vincent's tacked up—laughing at him in his chair. Vincent always makes Jimmy laugh. He's a fat crazy fuck, Jimmy thinks, but he's goddamned funny. And for years, Vincent's have been the only letters he's gotten.

Tijuana

Jimmy finds Rita passed out
in the bathroom of the bar
and hauls her outside. She walks
propped against him.
Sobers up on *chorizos*
from a street stand.
They drive Vincent's car
across the border,
a stiletto Jimmy bought
hidden in the air filter.
At a rest stop outside San Diego
Rita crouches in a field
under a million stars, puking.
The wind drags
through the weeds. Jimmy
fools with the radio,
gets a gospel show.
They drive back to Vincent's
and fix in the kitchen.
Vincent's making pancakes
from breadcrumbs and eggs,
reciting his poems
until Jimmy says *Shut up.*
Later in the yard
Rita's alone, rocking
and holding herself.
Jimmy comes to the window and stands there.
She thinks of the men
watching her from the doorways
of bars down south, how they acted
like all they had to do
was call to her. But Jimmy
just stands there,
smoking, looking at nothing.

PART THREE

Workout

Hitting the heavy bag
in the basement of Chumley's
mother's house, punching
until his bad knee gives out
and his trunks are soaked.
Then he just pushes it
with a glove, letting it swing.
When they'd returned
from Vincent's, he packed
a duffel. Rita
clinging to his knees and crying.
He'd had to kick her off
like a dog. Then he turned
and held her. What she did
to him he couldn't explain.
When she calmed down
he put her to bed
and left. Walked
all night around the city,
seeing men sleeping
on newspapers, cardboard,
sometimes with shopping carts
or puppies beside them.
He and Rita had eaten
at Saint Anthony's and seen
the same faces. More
and more people on the streets.
Even women—he found one
under the freeway, sitting up
with a two-by-four, afraid
to sleep. The next morning he'd knocked
at Chumley's. Every evening
(the worst time of day)
he laces the gloves tight

over wrapped hands
and goes at it until
he's too tired
to feel. It's not Rita
he sees, throwing hooks
and right crosses at the twisting
bag, jabbing the leather
where the face would be.

Afternoon

She keeps dreaming she's
at home again. Drops her schoolbooks
on the kitchen table,
opens the refrigerator for milk. Calling
for her mother. Checking the hall closet—
she'd found her there once,
crouched with a knife. *Don't be scared.*
No one's here. Her brothers
playing catch in the yard,
sister at a neighbor's.
Rita would hunt for money
to buy groceries,
shape hamburger meat
into small patties.
In the dream
she keeps opening doors,
pushing aside coats.
But she doesn't find anything.
(That last time, calling *Mama,*
opening the bathroom door—
the tub water rose-colored,
still warm, but she wouldn't wake.)
Her brothers' baseball flies up,
hits the empty house.

Moonflower

On the couch at Chumley's
he sleeps as late as he can,
then has to get through
the hours until night.
The day pushes him down
but in the dark he blooms—
fresh white shirt,
sleeves rolled up, a woman
letting him buy her drinks
and sometimes taking him home.
Thighs opening,
sharp odor of some perfume.
(Once he went back
to their old room
at the res hotel,
but Rita had gone, no one
could say where.)
Shapes around him
in the strange dark:
framed photographs,
their books,
objects from lives
he doesn't want to know about.
He always gets out before dawn,
slips money from their purses,
rides the bus through gray streets
when no one's up—
the world still and peaceful,
not yet the world.

Smaller Each Day

I don't have hands now.
Or a face, or anything else
he would recognize me by.
I have a sheet
that's sometimes clean,
a room I bring them to.
Cinderblock walls
and the smells
that make me sick later.
The men finish
and I go into the bathroom
and look at myself
disappearing where
they touched me.
At night I feel my heart
beating too hard
and I'm afraid.
Stop, I tell it.
But it keeps on
saying *Rita, Rita, Rita*
as if she'll answer.

Arrest

I guess it was Chumley's fault.
Not the first part,
that was both of us
looking for the right person
to take off, well-dressed guy,
seemed drunk, seemed like somebody
you could part from his wallet
easy, not even needing
a piece. But then he screamed,
maybe because Chumley had
to hit him,
and then Chumley had to show the gun
to shut him up. Except
he screamed again,
and even though we'd got
the money by then and should
have run, Chumley had to punch
him again
Shut up Shut up,
Don't you see what this is?
Shut up or I'll waste you,
like he was pissed
the guy wouldn't listen.
Chumley. Man, let's go.
I was afraid
he'd use it (thinking why was it
I was always pulling Chumley
off somebody, like that cop's
son, would have iced him that night
if I wasn't there)
Fuck it, come on
but by that time there were cars
and lights, and the guy
still yelling

so that even the cops
(Chumley slammed against the brick wall
and cuffed, patted down—
What else you got, you fuckin punk?)
told him to Shut
the fuck up.

Inside

dinner tray	cigarette	cement yard	stars
walls	magazine	cigarette	sleep
dreams	walls	spoons	tattoos
cigarette	shadow	toilet	cement yard
guards	movie	cigarette	sleep
toothbrush	photograph	harmonica	walls
dinner tray	cigarette	cement yard	stars

Bird

He finds it in the yard
one morning. Small, stunned,
still breathing. But before
he can do anything
(what could he do?)
T.J. and Spoon squat
down next to him. T.J.
flips it over: dark eyes,
legs drawn up. Spoon takes it
and hurls it at the fence.
Fly, you sucker, he says.

Linoleum

Once Jimmy had worked
at a factory on Mulberry Street.
Lifting the stacked squares
from skid to presser,
smell of asbestos
and sweat, the Polish foreman
bald like his father—
same thin strands combed
over a wide skull.
His father used to let him sip whiskey
from the silver thermos
in his lunchbox.
The foreman started in drinking
first thing, so afternoons
everything slowed—
Jimmy would daydream
escape, a fast car,
his arm around a woman.
Who cared where they went?
Prison is different, slower
and he doesn't daydream.
After two years he had quit
the factory, hitched to Arizona
and gradually worked his way
west, to this edge.
He can step off
or turn around.
There's no one to watch
him or care.
(Lifting the stacked squares.
A fast car, the wheel humming
under his hands, a woman
leaning her head
against his shoulder.) *Rita.*

Ward

On the wall a white crab
slowly turning to a skeleton,
the way clouds
change in the sky.
Then the bats—
they always come, not
swooping but floating
like big flakes of ash.
Shaking, she waits
for Jimmy to come back
from Diane's with the Valium.
Or was that
her father, standing there
in his blue pajamas
saying *Take this*
hours or minutes
before the black wings
brushed her cheek like kisses.

She opens her eyes.
Someone lifts her wrist,
presses a thumb
to the faint throbbing
beneath her skin.
I'm in here, she thinks.
For days the shape
on the wall holds,
then thins to pale smoke
that shreds in daylight.

Spin

After the hospital, her brother Jack comes and takes her to his house in Nevada City. It's small, he's working to buy it. His wife Donna bakes things all day, sells them to local restaurants. Rita eats brownies and watches TV, Donna comes in during the soaps and they sit together. Someone's always dying, falling in love, breaking up. Donna's pregnant. Rita helps her sometimes, sometimes just stays on the couch all day. Jack works as a roofer and some days he's there too. He rolls fat joints and they all giggle and eat too much. The only alcohol in the house is Jack's beer. For a week she won't touch it, but one night there's a sad movie on TV. She gets Jack a beer, then takes one for herself. After the movie Donna goes to bed. Rita and Jack stay up drinking, go outside and look up at the stars. She spins around, falls down laughing.

Bars are all the same, like men. She goes home with someone, fucks him. Goes someplace different the next night so she won't see him. But one bar she likes. She goes home with the bartender more than anyone and finally just him. He asks her to move in. That lasts a month, then she's back at Jack's. Donna wants her to leave, she says the baby needs quiet and so does she. Why don't you do something besides park your ass on my couch and drink all day, the least you could do is help out. Rita brings men in late. Someone falls over a chair, drinks Jack's beer, gets into a pie Donna was going to sell. One night Rita's standing naked against the refrigerator with somebody, Donna comes in and screams at her. Little whore. Good-for-nothing trash. The next day Jack tells her she has to leave. They go to the bank and he gives her some money, then drives off and leaves her there.

Outside

Still on probation,
he's careful,
won't touch anything that looks
like it might break bad.
He gets a job
washing dishes.
The guys he works with
are all right—Mexicans, Salvadorans.
Their English is bad. He likes
picking up words, teaching them.
Pussy is *coño*, he knows that
from prison, and like prison they say it
fifty times a day.

The kitchen is steam
and scalding water, yellow gloves
for his hands. On breaks
he sometime stands
just inside the restaurant,
leans against the wall
by the swinging door.
White tablecloths, bottles
in silver buckets,
fresh flowers everywhere.
No one looks at him.
He thinks about sitting there,
holding a menu. Then goes
out back to the alley
where he can smoke,
look up between buildings
and not be bothered.

Blues

No one knows where Diane is. I went there but she's gone. I went down the hall, looked at the door to our old apartment, thought about him.

Sometimes I sleep on the streets but it scares me. The shelter's better, it's all women, and people there don't treat you like dirt. Sometimes we put chairs in a circle and sit with a worker, everybody tells who they are. I say my name. Lots of them have babies. I'm lucky, I don't think I can have any.

I used to have a picture but I lost it. Jimmy playing one of his harmonicas, hair in his face. I pass somebody on a corner, playing by himself, a cigar box for money in front of him. I stand there and listen until a few people stop, then I move into a doorway.

Dancing

It's better than being a whore—
no one touches her.
She can't even see them,
dim faces behind glass.
She watches herself
in the mirrors,
thinks *I must be pretty.*
She's supposed to smile
all the time, but it's hard.
Relax and enjoy it,
Nicole tells her. Nicole's been there
a year. She has a snake
tattooed around her ankle,
short spiky hair she hides
under a wig,
a pierced nipple.
Rita asks if it hurt
and Nicole laughs.
*You're lucky you look
so sweet,* she says.
*They don't want to hire
any more like me.*
I'm sweet, Rita thinks,
sliding her hands down
her own hips, smiling
at nobody.

Window

I saw her on the street today.
She looked all right.
I wanted to get off the bus
but I was on my way to work
and couldn't be late
even for her. My boss says
I could make waiter someday.
Right now I'm still
in the kitchen, though.

I scrape off food and think
about her. How I couldn't make
her happy. How I'm tired
of having nothing
and nobody. This guy
I work with, Jorge—he sends money
to his family in Honduras.
He showed me their pictures.
He's got something.
I've got a room, a new TV.
I go home at night and sit there
like my old man used to.

She was standing in front
of a taqueria, leaning back against
the window glass.
She looked better than all right.
I couldn't tell if she was wearing
the ring I gave her. She had my name
engraved on the inside.
I rinse the dishes and silverware,
turn glasses upside down
on the scrubbing brush.
I do it all faster than the bus boys

can dump the dirty trays.
On break I go outside
and cry. *Only pussies cry,*
my old man used to say.
My old man,
who didn't know shit.

Shelter

It's noisy here. The kids run around, screaming, their mothers slap them and they cry. I have a bottom bunk, I hang a blanket from the bed above me for privacy. In the middle of the night it's finally quiet. I lie awake and think about goals. Sheryl, the worker, says I need some. She says What do you want Rita? and I say peace and quiet, maybe someplace sunnier than here. I say I'd like to have a dog. A big one, a retriever or shepherd with long soft fur. What else? she says. I remember my dad's garden, how I used to like sitting with him while he weeded, putting my toes in the dirt. He grew tomatoes, corn, peas. There was a rosebush, too, once he let me pick a big rose and there was a spider in it, I got scared and shook it and the petals went all over me and he laughed. He showed me how to put my thumb over the hoze nozzle so it sprayed. Sheryl says I could garden. I think about the coleus Jimmy and I had, how I would take cuttings, put them in water and they'd grow more flowers. But then they all died. At night I listen to everybody sleep around me, some people snoring, some starting to say something and then stopping. It's pitch-dark behind the blanket. I try to see it sunny, a yard with a dog lying down under a tree. I try to smell warm tomatoes. Curl my toes in the sheets. Try to sleep.

Rita's Dream

We're in a bar together.
It's dark but there's a mirrored ball
in the middle of the ceiling.
Somebody moved the pool table,
it's like a dance floor. Jimmy's
wearing a suit jacket,
the one from our wedding.
Some women from the shelter
are looking for their babies.
One's in the dumpster and everyone goes
outside to look. Then I'm in
the bathroom, a man's in there and tries
to hand me a rat, it's big and dark,
slippery, I won't take it, I run out
to find Jimmy again. We dance
and I smell his cologne and feel safe.
Some kind of fight is happening,
someone says *Fuck you* loud
and then *Get away, get away.*
But we just keep dancing.
My dad takes our picture and the flash
makes me close my eyes,
and when I open them
Jimmy is looking at me and I know
he loves me, I know
he isn't ever going to stop.

Acknowledgments

I wish to thank San Francisco State University for a Summer Stipend which enabled me to complete an early draft of this work, as well as the Djerassi Foundation in Woodside, California, where I wrote a portion of the book. I'm also very grateful to Thom Ward and Steve Huff at BOA for their insightful comments and suggestions for revision, and to my editor, Al Poulin, Jr., for his faith in me.

In addition, I'm greatly indebted to the National Endowment for the Arts, for money that encouraged and literally supported me. Without that help, this book might have remained unwritten.

Finally, thanks to the people whose love keeps me going, especially my mother, Dorianne, Aya, and Joey.

Lyrics from "Sweet Little Bullet from a Pretty Blue Gun," by Tom Waits, © 1978 by Fifth Floor Music, used by permission.

About the Author

Kim Addonizio was born in Washington, DC, in 1954 and now lives in California. She holds a master's degree in creative writing from San Francisco State University. Her first poetry collection, *The Philosopher's Club* (BOA), received The 1994 Great Lakes New Writers Award and a Silver Medal from the Commonwealth Club of California. She is co-author, with Dorianne Laux, of *The Poet's Companion: A Guide to the Pleasures of Writing Poetry* (W.W. Norton & Co., 1997), and the recipient of two fellowships from the National Endowment for the Arts, and a Pushcart Prize.

BOA EDITIONS, LTD.: AMERICAN POETS CONTINUUM SERIES